Baby
— AND —
Toddler
Food

KÖNEMANN

COOKING FOR YOUR CHILD

Preparing quick, nourishing meals for your baby or toddler is not difficult, even for a busy mother.

Sometimes the thought of preparing food for a baby about to be weaned from breast or bottle can be very daunting—particularly if cooking isn't really one of your great talents. But with a little thought and planning, nourishing tasty food is not difficult to achieve, even for the first-time mother (and cook).

Commercial baby foods are designed to be convenient and they are just that. They are not intended to replace every meal. They lack the texture necessary to stimulate chewing skills, don't help your baby learn about taste and flavor and can prove expensive.

You will notice that after up to six months of thriving on breast or bottle milk, your baby needs more food more often. Babies are individuals with differing needs, so there can be no hard and fast rules about this important step, but usually by four to six months you will begin experimenting with solid food. It is important not to introduce solid food too early as your baby's digestive system may not yet be ready.

When you feel that it is time for solid feeding to begin, usually around the fifth or sixth month, your baby may be growing quickly and be happy to receive the extra nourishment. But many babies still do not, at this stage, require more than milk alone. It will be a time of experimentation for both of you and if, after several attempts, your baby is not interested, delay it for another few weeks.

First solids should be nutritious to allow for normal, happy development and to help resist disease. Rice cereal is the traditional first food and gradually new tastes and textures are introduced. Try one at a time, in small amounts, even if your baby seems to love the taste. Allow for individual preferences and don't worry if at times your baby isn't interested in what you are offering—it isn't a criticism of your cooking. Remember, providing your baby is in good health, these meals are only a minor part of his daily diet, which will still consist mainly of milk. Your baby will enjoy and should be able to tolerate several different foods in the early weeks of spoon feeding. Well-ripened fruit, such as bananas, are easier to digest. Mashed with a fork and mixed with a little cereal or juice, they are perfect. Gradually increase the thickness and texture as your baby learns to chew.

Within two months of introducing solid foods, your child's consumption may have increased to as much as six or eight tablespoons of solids daily, including a number of different foods. By this time he may be enjoying three meals a day. Variety in the diet is not yet important. He would probably be content with the same foods at each meal. You can start selecting new foods to interest him, however.

When it comes to meal preparation for baby, the appliances that are helpful are the freezer, microwave and blender. It doesn't mean you have to run out and purchase any of these items (an ordinary potato masher can be used to purée soft food such as cooked pumpkin) but if you have them, use them.

Before you know it, your baby will be eating three meals a day along with the rest of the family and you'll be wondering where the time went. Introducing your child to solid food should be fun. Enjoying each new stage of your baby's development is all part of the joy of parenting.

milk

Breast milk is undoubtedly the most nutritious food for a new baby, however, for various reasons some women find themselves unable to breastfeed. This can be a very distressing situation, both for mother and child, and must be handled under advice from professionals.

■ Advice on breastfeeding can be provided by your pediatrician, a breastfeeding counselor, or from postpartum support groups like the La Leche League. If bottle feeding is deemed necessary, there are strict guidelines which need to be followed in the preparation of bottles to prevent illness or undernutrition of your baby. Your doctor will direct you on which formula to use and how often to feed.

■ Cow's milk is not an alternative as a main food source, but can be used, boiled, in the preparation of solid food for children over 9 months.

■ After thorough washing, all bottles, nipples, nipple covers and other bottle parts must be sterilized. This can be done by boiling all parts for 5 minutes, or immersing in a diluted sterilizing solution according to the manufacturer's instructions, or in a microwave or electric sterilizing unit. Do not rinse after sterilizing.

■ Hands must be scrupulously clean before preparing bottles. Make up the formula directly into the bottle, according to the manufacturer's instructions. Measure accurately, using the scoop provided. The water must have boiled for 5 minutes, then cooled to the correct temperature. Refrigerate the bottles immediately.

■ For convenience, rinse bottles and nipples immediately after use, then wash and sterilize all at one time. The pieces may be left in the sterilizing solution until needed. You can make up to a day's supply of bottles, but they must be used within 24 hours.

■ When ready to feed, warm the bottle by standing it in a pan of hot water for a couple of minutes. The milk should never be hot, just warm or with the chill from the refrigerator taken off. Test the temperature by shaking a few drops onto your wrist. Always err on the side of caution. Don't heat bottles in the microwave. The milk may heat unevenly and have 'hot spots', even if it feels OK when tested.

■ If your baby refuses the bottle, try a different teat. It is not usually the formula that is disliked.

■ Always make sure you are following the guidelines correctly. It is very important to do this—each year in the US, 20,000 infants are admitted to hospital with gastroenteritis.

■ Some breastfeeding mothers find that eating spicy foods, chocolate, alcohol, tea or fruit juice can upset their baby.

■ Traveling, or even a day out, with a bottle-fed baby can be tricky. The bottle must be kept chilled, then warmed to feed. Formula should never be kept at room temperature. The bottle must be kept in an insulated bag, but you will be at the mercy of busy restaurant staff or shopkeepers to reheat it for you.

■ A good tip is to put the boiled water into the bottle while it is warm and make up the formula when you get to your destination. Depending on the time elapsed, the water will be around room temperature, which is quite acceptable for your baby to drink.

■ Rather than traveling with a large can of formula, ready-to-pour liquid formulas come in various sizes including single-feed size. If your budget allows, you may want to consider formulas that are not only pre-prepared, but sealed in throwaway bottles.

■ Your baby will begin with small, frequent feeds. Gradually the number of feeds per day will decrease, while the quantity taken at each feed will increase—up to a point. When solids are established the milk feeds become secondary.

first

Your baby will probably be ready for solids around four to six months—earlier than four months, her digestive system will be too immature to tolerate them. When she is ready she will be happy to receive the extra nourishment and will let you know by reaching for food and by making chewing movements.

■ Rice cereal is the best choice for the firs solid food as it is easy to digest. Dilute it with breast milk, cooled boiled water or formula. For nursing babies the breast milk will give the first cereal a familiar taste and smell—after several days you could change to formula and water.

■ The cereal should not be runny and you may have more success by making it quite thick. Use a very small spoon and only half fill it. Even if your baby loves the food, do not give her more than a couple of spoonfuls at these early feeds.

■ The best time to try first solids is at the mid-morning feed when your baby is settled and in a cooperative mood.

■ Never feed your baby cereal from a bottle using a nipple with an enlarged hole. If she will not take it from a spoon, try later.

■ Trying to give her solids at the end of the feed may be pointless as she will be satisfied by the milk, unless she has developed a strong urge for extra nourishment. It is wisest not to offer new solids at the night-time feed as a bad reaction may lead to a sleepless night.

■ Serve food at room temperature—if you want to take the chill off it, place the dish over a cup of very hot water to warm slightly. Always check the temperature before serving.

foods

■ Remember that your baby's swallowing has been associated with sucking until now. At first she may cough, splutter and spit food out. Be very patient and give very small amounts each time. If she coughs or sneezes, hold a hand in front of her face, not over her mouth.

■ If you have offered your baby food and she has rejected it, do not save it for the next meal—if any saliva has touched the food, bacteria may grow.

■ Once your baby is enjoying cereal you can offer her small amounts of puréed fruit and vegetables. Mash the boiled vegetables with a fork or push them through a sieve and then dilute to a soft purée with a little boiled water or formula.

■ Fresh fish is excellent for babies over six months—be very careful that all the skin and bones are removed.

■ Keep it simple. Your baby won't appreciate elaborate meals and you won't appreciate the stress of preparing them.

■ Make fresh fruit gelatine dessert by setting diluted fruit juice with gelatine. You will need 3 teaspoons of gelatine (dissolved in 3 tablespoons boiling water) for every 2 cups of juice.

■ Your baby has no craving for sugar, salt and cream so think of her future eating habits and don't add extra sweetness or fat. Babies get the fat that they need from milk.

■ Remember, milk is the most important food for your baby in her first year. If she is leaving some formula in the bottle or cutting her breast feeding time short, it may mean that she is being satisfied by solids.

food

We know more about food allergies these days and so can take better precautions to avoid them—the following hints will provide you with some commonsense guidelines. The recipes in this book are written for healthy children without known allergies but it is always sensible to be aware of possible problem foods.

■ Allergies usually involve only one or two foods and mainly affect children with a family background of conditions such as asthma, hay fever and eczema. True food allergy only occurs in less than 10 per cent of children. **Babies with eczema are the ones most at risk of having food allergies.**

■ Foods like cow's milk, soy and egg can cause allergies in some babies if they are given before four months of age. Breast feeding cannot prevent allergies but it can help. The most allergic babies will still have reactions unless the breast feeding mother changes her diet.

■ Severe allergies to food are rare and usually obvious—they can cause itching and swelling (usually around the mouth), vomiting and cramps, often within minutes. Milder reactions include spots or rashes on the skin, vomiting, diarrhea, runny nose, wheezing and coughing, or asthma. As some of these are obviously similar to a common cold it is best to consult your doctor rather than immediately assume an allergy.

■ If you have been introducing new foods one at a time it should be quite easy to work out which is the problem food and avoid it in future. If your baby does react to a food, always consult your doctor about how to deal with the problem. Don't try the problem food again without medical supervision—. allergies should always be taken very seriously.

allergies

■ The foods which most commonly cause reactions include eggs (particularly egg whites), cow's milk, fish and peanuts. An allergy to cow's milk makes it impossible to wean a baby from breast to most formulas, as well as cow's milk. Soy bean milk may be the answer, but always consult your doctor.

■ Because of the danger of choking, don't give whole or chopped nuts to children under seven years.

■ Children tend to grow out of allergies to egg, milk, wheat and soy by the age of five or six, though sometimes a particular food such as fish or peanuts can cause problems for life.

■ If your toddler has a food allergy and is going to a party, call the hosts beforehand and let them know what food your child cannot have. Give your toddler something to eat and drink before going to the party.

■ Make sure that anyone who may prepare or buy food for your child (grandparents, childminder) knows about an allergy.

■ Food intolerances are more common than food allergies and can occur at any time during life. They are due to chemicals in foods which have a lot of natural or artificial flavor, such as sweets, cordial, fruit juice, strawberries, dried fruit, honey and chocolate.

■ The amount of food chemicals can build up in the body from a variety of foods. Symptoms only occur when the total amount is higher than the child can tolerate. Symptoms vary from person to person, but may include irritability, hyperactivity, skin rashes, leg pains and headaches. To control symptoms, the quantity of problem foods will need to be reduced.

FIRST FOODS FOR BABIES 4–9 MONTHS

Cereal—easy to swallow and digest—is the traditional first food. All recipes serve one baby unless stated.

RICE CEREAL

Combine 1 teaspoon rice cereal with enough breast milk/formula or boiled water to produce a thick consistency.

SHREDDED WHEAT

Crush a quarter of a Shredded Wheat biscuit and mix with a little breast milk, formula or boiled water to produce the desired consistency.

OATMEAL

Combine 1 tablespoon rolled oats and 1 tablespoon cold water. Stir in 1 1/2 tablespoons hot water. Bring to the boil, stirring, and then reduce the heat and simmer for 1 minute. Purée with enough breast milk or formula to produce the consistency required.

POACHED FRUIT

Peel, core and slice 1 apple, peach or pear and put in a small pan with 2 tablespoons water. Bring to the boil, reduce the heat and simmer until soft and pulpy, adding more water as required. Purée with a little boiled water to make $1/2$ cup of fruit.

RICE CEREAL AND POACHED FRUIT

Combine 1 teaspoon rice cereal with 1 teaspoon poached fruit or mashed banana. Add enough breast milk, formula or boiled water to produce a soft, but not runny, cereal.

BABY CEREAL WITH FRUIT AND YOGURT

For older babies, mix together baby cereal, poached fruit, baby yogurt and breast milk, formula or boiled water to produce the desired consistency.

Ideas for purées
Always purée using breast milk, formula or boiled water.
■ Mashed avocado and cottage cheese.
■ Sieved tomato and avocado. Peel and seed the tomatoes before pressing them through a sieve. Peel tomatoes by cutting a cross in the top and plunging them into boiling water for 1 minute. Refresh in cold water and the skin will easily peel away. Quarter, then remove the seeds with a spoon.
■ Mashed ripe banana and strained orange juice.
■ Puréed apple, pear and banana.
■ Cottage cheese and poached fruit.
■ Creamed potato.
■ Puréed pumpkin.
■ Puréed potato, pumpkin and zucchini.
■ Puréed sweet potato and avocado.
■ Puréed potato, baked beans and cottage cheese or grated mild cheese.
■ Puréed spinach and cheese sauce.
■ Puréed vegetable soup.
■ Vegetables and well-cooked meat, puréed.
■ Puréed vegetables and cooked fish.

TOAST FINGERS
Butter 1 slice of toast and cut into fingers for an older baby.

HOME-MADE TEETHING BISCUITS
Remove the crusts from 5 thick slices of stale bread. Cut the bread into fingers. Put the bread on a baking sheet and bake in a very slow oven (250°F) for 1 hour or until dry and hard. Allow to cool thoroughly and store in an airtight container. Makes about 20.

PUREED VEGETABLES
Put 1/2 cup peeled and chopped vegetables in a steamer basket over a saucepan of gently simmering water, cover tightly and steam until tender. Purée with a little breast milk, formula or boiled water.

Note: Don't ever heat baby's milk or feeds in the microwave: some areas can become very hot while others remain cool.

Clockwise from top left: *Toast Fingers; Cheese Sauce with Vegetables; Vegetable Soup; Puréed Vegetables; Teething Biscuits*

CHEESE SAUCE

Melt $^1/_2$ oz butter in a small saucepan. Mix in 2 teaspoons all-purpose flour and cook for 1 minute, stirring continuously. Remove from the heat and gradually blend in $^1/_2$ cup milk until smooth. Return to the heat and stir continuously until the sauce boils and thickens. Reduce the heat and simmer for 2 minutes. Blend in 2 tablespoons grated mild Cheddar cheese. This makes about $^1/_2$ cup of sauce which you can serve with boiled or mashed vegetables, or bread.

VEGETABLE SOUP

Put 2 cups water in a pan with 1 cup chopped mixed vegetables and 1 tablespoon rice. Bring to the boil, reduce the heat and simmer until the vegetables and rice are tender. Allow to cool and then purée before serving. Freeze or refrigerate any leftovers. You can give older babies croûtons.

TODDLER BREAKFASTS

For toddlers, as for adults, breakfast can be the most important meal of the day. All serve one unless stated.

CEREAL MIXTURES

Blend milk with rice cereal, yogurt and puréed or chopped fresh or dried fruit. Put the dish in a bowl of hot water and stir until warmed. Alternatively, warm in the microwave on Medium power, for 45 seconds, blending in more milk as required. Always test the temperature before serving.

TODDLER MUESLI

Mix together 1 cup rolled oats, $1/2$ cup mixed dried fruit (chopped or grated dried apple, apricot, pear or coconut), 2 crushed Shredded Wheat biscuits and 2 tablespoons oat bran. Store in an airtight container. Serve with a little milk.

Note: For fussy toddlers, add $1/2$ cup Rice Krispies, cornflakes or other favorite cereal.

FRUITY RICE

Mix together $1/2$ cup warm, cooked rice and $1/4$ cup chopped, fresh or dried fruit. Top with a dollop of natural yogurt.

Note: If your child is not yet chewing adequately, substitute puréed fruit for pieces. Flavored yogurt or yogurt dessert can be used instead of natural yogurt.

Top: *Instant Breakfast (left) and Oatmeal*
Below, from left: *Toddler Muesli; Fruity Rice; Fruit Mixtures; Cereal Mixtures*

INSTANT BREAKFAST

Rather than just pouring out a bowl of cereal, serve buttered slices of raisin bread and a mixture of sliced fresh fruit (kiwi, apple, pear, melon, strawberry) for a delicious instant breakfast.

OATMEAL

Prepare oatmeal as directed on the packet, with water or milk. Add chopped fresh fruit, dried fruit, puréed fruit, honey or brown sugar, for a warming breakfast.

FRUIT MIXTURES

Combine puréed, chopped fresh or dried fruit with yogurt. If you are using natural yogurt, drizzle with a little honey.

Toast Toppers

■ Toast 2 slices bread under a hot broiler until golden on both sides. Sprinkle with 1/2 cup grated mild Cheddar cheese and broil until the cheese melts. Slice into fingers. Toppings can be put on English muffins as well.

■ Top a slice of toast with a slice of tomato. Broil for about 1 minute and then sprinkle with grated cheese. Broil until the cheese melts and then slice into fingers.

■ Spread toast with mashed baked beans and sprinkle with grated cheese. Broil until the cheese melts and slice into fingers.

■ Mix together 1/2 cup grated cheese with 1/2 chopped tomato and 1 finely chopped slice of ham. Spread over a slice of toast and broil until the cheese melts. Slice into fingers.

■ Spread a slice of toast with mashed avocado. Sprinkle with grated cheese and broil until the cheese melts. Slice into fingers.

CHEESY EGGS

Melt 1 teaspoon butter in a small saucepan and cook 1 tablespoon peeled chopped tomato until tender. Whisk together 1 egg, 1 tablespoon milk and 1 tablespoon grated Cheddar cheese and add to the pan. Cook gently, stirring until thickened. Serve with toast or bread to toddlers who have started eating egg. Poached eggs are also easy and nutritious for toddlers. Poach in simmering water for 2–3 minutes.

BANANA SMOOTHIE

Put 1 cup milk, 2 tablespoons plain yogurt and 1 small ripe banana in a food processor and process until smooth. Add a little honey or sugar to sweeten if you like. Serve immediately with a straw.

MILK SHAKE

Put 1 cup milk, 1/3 cup vanilla yogurt and a few drops of vanilla extract in a food processor. Process until well combined and frothy. Serve immediately with a straw.

FRENCH TOAST

Beat an egg with a little milk. Cut a thick slice of white bread into squares and dip into the egg. Cook in a non-stick frying pan, brushed with a little oil or melted butter, until golden on both sides.

FRUITY DIP

Pour 1/2 cup flavored yogurt or yogurt dessert into a serving dish. Grate or cut a variety of fruit into small pieces (banana, pear, apple, kiwi fruit, pawpaw, strawberries or whatever is in season). Serve with the yogurt for dipping. You could use cottage cheese instead of yogurt.

Clockwise from top left:
Banana Smoothie;
Milk Shake; Fruity Dip;
French Toast; Cheesy Eggs

JUNIOR PIKELETS

Preparation: **10 minutes**
Cooking time: **20 minutes**
MAKES ABOUT **24**

1 cup self-rising
   flour
1/4 teaspoon
   baking soda
2 tablespoons sugar
1 egg
1/2 cup milk
2 teaspoons oil
1/2 cup golden raisins,
   optional

1 Sift the flour and
   soda together into a
bowl. Stir in the sugar.
2 Make a well in the
   center and whisk
in the combined egg,
milk and oil to make
a smooth batter.
Add the golden raisins
for children over
12 months old.
3 Heat and lightly
   grease a frying pan.
Drop teaspoons of the
batter into the pan and
cook until bubbles form.
Turn and cook the other
side until golden. Cool
on a wire rack. Serve
with butter. Can be
frozen, layered between
sheets of wax paper, for
up to 1 month.

MINI APPLE MUFFINS

Preparation: **10 minutes**
Cooking time: **15 minutes**
MAKES ABOUT **24**

2 cups all-purpose flour
1 tablespoon baking
   powder
1 teaspoon ground
   cinnamon
1/2 cup brown sugar
1 cup milk
4 oz butter, melted
1 egg, beaten
2 green apples, peeled,
   cored and grated

1 Preheat the oven to
   400°F. Sift the flour,
baking powder and
cinnamon into a bowl.
Stir in the sugar.
2 Make a well in the
   center and add the
combined milk, butter,
egg and apple. Blend
together, stirring no
more than 15 times.
3 Spoon into greased
   mini muffin pans
until 3/4 full. Bake for
15 minutes, or until
cooked and golden.
Cool on a wire rack
and store in an airtight
container. Muffins can
be frozen in a sealed
bag for up to 1 month.

CHEESY BRAN MUFFINS

Preparation: **10 minutes**
Cooking time: **15 minutes**
MAKES ABOUT **24**

2 cups all-purpose flour
1 tablespoon baking
   powder
1 cup grated Cheddar
   cheese
1/2 cup unprocessed
   bran
1 cup milk
4 oz butter, melted
1 egg, beaten

1 Preheat the oven to
   400°F. Sift the flour
and baking powder into
a bowl. Stir in the
cheese and bran.
2 Make a well in the
   center and add the
combined milk, butter
and egg. Fold together,
stirring no more than
15 times (the batter
will still be lumpy).
3 Spoon into greased
   mini muffin pans
until 3/4 full. Bake for
15 minutes, or until
golden. Cool on a wire
rack and store in an
airtight container.
Muffins can be frozen
in a sealed bag for up
to 1 month.

From top: *Junior Pikelets; Mini Apple Muffins;* ▶
Cheesy Bran Muffins

TODDLER LUNCHES

Lunchtime can be fun with these ideas for quick meals, so pull up a chair and enjoy your toddler's company.

SAUSAGE ROLLS

Preheat the oven to 400°F. Mix together 4 oz sausage meat with 4 oz ground steak, 1 tablespoon tomato ketchup and 2 teaspoons all-purpose flour. Form into a sausage shape. Place along one edge of a thawed sheet of ready-rolled puff pastry. Roll up and cut into short lengths. Place on a baking sheet. Brush with a little milk or beaten egg. Bake for 15–20 minutes. Serve with salad.

QUICK AS A WINK PIES

Preheat the oven to 400°F. Place leftover seasoned ground meat, meat casserole, bolognese sauce or sweet curry in the base of a small ramekin. Top with thawed, ready-rolled puff pastry (cut a small steam hole in the center). Brush with milk or beaten egg and bake for 15–20 minutes. Cool to serve.

MY FIRST SALAD

Children love food they can eat with their fingers, so salads are ideal. Try crisp lettuce leaves topped with grated carrot, tomato wedges, slices of cheese or cold cooked meats, and orange segments or chunks of kiwi fruit. Hard fruits like carrot or apple should be grated, not chopped, to prevent choking.

COTTAGE CHEESE AND CHICKEN

Mix together $1/2$ cup chopped cooked chicken, $1/2$ cup cottage cheese, half a tomato, chopped, and quarter of an avocado. Serve with bread and butter, toast fingers or pieces of roll. Alternatively, stir into cold, cooked pasta shells.

CHEESY BAKED BEANS

Peel and chop 1 potato and boil until very tender; drain. Add $4^1/2$ oz baked beans and $1/4$ cup grated mild Cheddar or cottage cheese. Purée or mash with a little milk and serve warm with bread and butter.

AVOCADO DIP

Mix together half an avocado, $1/4$ cup grated mild Cheddar cheese and quarter of a tomato, chopped. Purée or mash the mixture well. You could also add a few drops of French dressing. Serve with toast fingers.

From left: *Sausage Rolls; Cheesy Baked Beans; Quick as a Wink Pies; My First Salad; Cottage Cheese and Chicken; Avocado Dip*

LOTS OF SANDWICHES

Use a variety of breads (such as flour tortillas, pita, buns, bagels, whole wheat and so on) for making sandwiches and serve with milk or diluted fruit juice for a quick nutritious lunch. Try these for fillings:

- ham and cheese
- egg and tomato
- taramasalata and lettuce
- hummus and bean sprouts
- cold cooked ham or chicken and tomato
- cold cooked rissoles or sausage with tomato sauce
- Marmite, cheese and cucumber
- cottage cheese, grated carrot and avocado

BITS AND PIECES WITH DIP

Arrange small slices of cheese, cold cooked meat, salad, vegetables such as seeded cucumber or chopped tomatoes, fruit and bread sticks on a plate. Serve with a quick and easy lunchtime dip such as yogurt flavored with mashed avocado, cottage cheese or hummus.

Note: It may be tempting for busy mothers, but never leave children alone while they are eating. Sticks of hard raw vegetables and fruit such as carrot or apple are only suitable for older children— they should be grated, cooked or mashed for younger children and toddlers. Always remove any skin and seeds which could cause choking. Make sure children sit quietly while they eat—running, playing, laughing or crying while eating can lead to choking.

SAVORY FLAN

Preparation: **15 minutes**
Cooking time: **45 minutes**
SERVES **8**

1 1/2 cups grated cheese
4 oz ricotta cheese
4 oz ham, chopped or
2 slices rindless
   lean bacon, broiled
   and chopped
1 zucchini, grated
1 tablespoon chopped
   fresh parsley
3 eggs
1 1/2 cups milk

1 Preheat the oven to
350°F. Mix together
the cheeses, ham or
bacon, zucchini and
parsley. Place in the
base of a greased 9 inch
flan dish or pie plate.

2 Whisk together the
eggs and milk and
pour into the dish.

3 Bake for 40–45
minutes, or until set
and golden brown.

TUNA MORNAY

Preparation: **10 minutes**
Cooking time: **5 minutes**
SERVES **2**

1/2 oz butter
2 teaspoons all-
   purpose flour
1/2 cup milk
1/4 cup grated
   cheese
6 oz canned tuna
1 tablespoon chopped
   parsley, optional

1 Melt the butter in a
small pan. Add the
flour and cook, stirring
constantly, over low
heat for 1 minute.

2 Gradually add the
milk, stirring the
mixture until smooth
between each addition.
When all the milk has
been added, keep
stirring until the
mixture has boiled and
thickened. Cook for
1 minute longer.

3 Remove from the
heat and stir in the
cheese until melted.
Drain the tuna and
flake with a fork. Stir
into the sauce with the
parsley. Serve warm,
with bread.

FISH PATTIES

Preparation: **15 minutes**
Cooking time: **15 minutes**
MAKES **4**

1 small boneless fish
1 potato, cooked and
   mashed
1/4 cup grated carrot
1/4 cup grated zucchini
1/4 cup grated Cheddar
   cheese
1/4 cup all-purpose flour
olive oil

1 Steam, poach or
microwave the fish
and break into flakes,
checking carefully for
bones or skin. Mix
together with the
potato, carrot, zucchini
and cheese.

2 Shape into small
patties or fingers and
dust with flour. Lightly
brush a non-stick pan
with olive oil and cook
the patties slowly until
golden brown. Turn
once during cooking.

3 Drain well on paper
towels and serve
with wedges of tomato.

◀ **From top:** *Savory Flan; Tuna Mornay; Fish Patties*

VEGGIE PUFFS

Preparation: **15 minutes**
Cooking time: **15 minutes**
MAKES **24**

1 small potato,
  finely chopped
1 small carrot, finely
  chopped
1 small zucchini,
  chopped
1 stalk celery, chopped
1/4 cup chopped
  pumpkin
1/4 cup chopped
  broccoli
1/4 cup chopped
  cauliflower
2 cups grated cheese
2 sheets puff pastry,
  halved
milk, for coating

1 Put the potato,
carrot, zucchini,
celery, pumpkin,
broccoli and
cauliflower in a small
saucepan and add
enough water to cover
them. Bring to the boil,
then reduce the heat
and simmer for
3 minutes. Drain well
and transfer to a bowl
to cool. Add the cheese
to the vegetables and
mix well.

2 Preheat the oven to
425°F. Put the
four pieces of pastry out
on a board, divide the
mixture in four and
spread it along the long
side of each piece.

3 Roll up the pastry to
form sausage shapes,
brush the edge with a
little milk and press to
seal. Place the rolls,
seam side down, on a
lightly greased baking
sheet. Make a few small
slits along the rolls.

4 Lightly brush the
rolls with milk to
glaze and then bake for
10 minutes, or until
crisp and golden. Cut
each roll into 6 even-
sized pieces using a
sharp knife.

MUFFIN PIZZAS

Preparation: **10 minutes**
Cooking time: **5 minutes**
SERVES **2**

1 English muffin,
  halved
1 tablespoon tomato
  ketchup
1/4 cup chopped ham
1/4 cup sliced pineapple
1/2 cup grated
  mozzarella cheese

1 Spread each muffin
half with tomato
sauce. Top with ham
and pineapple and
sprinkle with cheese.

2 Broil until the
cheese melts. Serve
with a small salad.

OMELET

Preparation: **5 minutes**
Cooking time: **5 minutes**
SERVES **1**

1 egg
1 tablespoon milk
1 teaspoon butter
fillings such as cottage
  cheese, leftover
  vegetables, chopped
  cooked bacon,
  chopped tomato,
  sliced mushrooms or
  grated cheese

1 Whisk together the
egg and milk. Melt
the butter in a small
frying pan and add the
egg mixture, swirling to
cover the pan.

2 When the omelet is
almost set sprinkle
the filling over it. Fold
in half to enclose the
filling. Cook 1 minute
more. Slide onto a
plate and allow to cool.

From top: *Muffin Pizzas; Veggie Puffs; Omelet* ▶

SAVORY SHELLS

Preparation: **10 minutes**
Cooking time: **10 minutes**
SERVES 1

1/2 oz butter
1/4 cup chopped
  mushrooms
2 teaspoons
  all-purpose flour
1/2 cup milk
1/4 cup cottage cheese
1/4 cup grated mild
  Cheddar cheese
1 small tomato, peeled,
  seeded and chopped
1/2 cup cooked pasta
  shells

1 Melt the butter in a small saucepan and sauté the mushrooms until tender.

2 Stir in the flour and cook for 1 minute. Remove from the heat and gradually blend in the milk, stirring all the time until smooth.

3 Return to the heat. Cook, stirring continuously, until the sauce boils and thickens. Reduce the heat and simmer for 3 minutes.

4 Blend in the cheeses and tomato then gently mix through the pasta shells and serve.

APRICOT DRUMS

Preparation: **35 minutes**
Cooking time: **30 minutes**
SERVES 4

4 chicken drumsticks
1/4 cup apricot nectar
1 tablespoon soy sauce
2 teaspoons tomato
  ketchup
1 teaspoon lemon juice

1 Make a few slashes in each chicken drumstick, using a sharp knife. (For younger toddlers, remove the skin.) Put the drumsticks in a shallow ovenproof dish.

2 Pour over the combined nectar, sauces, lemon juice. Set aside to marinate for about 30 minutes, basting occasionally.

3 Preheat the oven to 350°F and bake, with the marinade, for 30 minutes or until tender, turning once. Serve with rice. Remove the chicken from the bone for younger toddlers. Any extra cooked chicken can be covered and refrigerated for up to one day.

MINI MEAT PATTIES

Preparation: **10 minutes**
Cooking time: **20 minutes**
MAKES 8

1 lb lean ground
  steak
1 onion, grated
1 potato, grated
1 carrot, grated
1 egg, beaten
1/4 cup golden raisins
1/4 cup fresh
  bread crumbs
2 tablespoons tomato
  ketchup
olive oil

1 Mix together all the ingredients and shape into 8 even-sized, flat patties. (If you don't want to cook all the patties, wrap them individually in plastic wrap and freeze for up to 6 months.)

2 Heat a little oil in a frying pan. Cook the patties, in batches if necessary, over medium heat for about 5 minutes each side. Serve with steamed or raw vegetables and mashed potatoes.

◀ **From top:** *Mini Meat Patties; Apricot Drums; Savory Shells*

CREAMED RICE

Preparation: **5 minutes**
Cooking time: **25 minutes**
SERVES 4

1 oz butter
1 cup short-grain rice
1/4 teaspoon ground
   cinnamon
2 1/2 cups milk
1/4 cup sugar
1/4 cup golden raisins
   optional

1 Melt the butter in a
pan and sauté the
rice and cinnamon for
1 minute.

2 Stir in the milk and
sugar and bring to
the boil. Reduce the
heat and simmer,
stirring occasionally, for
20 minutes, or until the
rice is tender.

3 Blend in the golden
raisins (for older
toddlers). Serve with
fresh fruit.

BAKED CUSTARD

Preparation: **5 minutes**
Cooking time: **20 minutes**
SERVES 2

1 1/2 cups milk
2 eggs
1 tablespoon sugar
few drops vanilla
   extract
ground nutmeg

1 Preheat the oven to
350°F. Whisk
together the milk, eggs,
sugar and vanilla
extract. Pour into
2 ramekins or a small
ovenproof dish and
sprinkle with a little
ground nutmeg.

2 Stand the ramekins
or casserole dish in
an oven pan. Fill the
pan with warm water to
come halfway up the
side of the dish.

3 Bake for about
15–20 minutes
(35–40 minutes for the
larger dish). When
cooked, the point of a
knife inserted into the
centre of the custard
will come out clean
and dry. Remove the
dish from the water and
allow to cool.

FRUIT KEBABS WITH HONEY AND YOGURT

Preparation: **15 minutes**
Cooking time: **Nil**
MAKES 4

8 strawberries, hulled
1 banana, chopped
1 kiwi fruit, peeled
   and chopped
1/2 small pineapple,
   peeled and chopped
1/4 cantaloupe, seeded
   and chopped
6 1/2 natural yogurt
2 tablespoons honey

1 Thread pieces of
fruit alternately onto
4 popsicle sticks.

2 Blend together the
yogurt and honey
and serve as a dipping
sauce for the fruit.

Note: Always toss
banana (or apple and
pear) in lemon juice if
leaving cut for any
length of time or else
it will discolor.

From top: *Creamed Rice; Baked Custard;* ▶
Fruit Kebabs with Honey and Yogurt

kitchen

Meal times are usually very busy times in many homes, so for most of us the aim is to prepare foods that the whole family, including baby, will enjoy. This need not be hard work, but does require a little planning and thought. If you have a freezer, microwave and blender, these can all be put to good use.

■ There are not many foods that cannot be frozen—and those that can't should be prepared in smaller quantities and stored in the refrigerator. Always make a little extra so that you have left-overs for tomorrow's dinner or to freeze for a 'meal in a hurry'.

■ Freeze single serves of purées in an ice cube tray or by simply dropping spoonfuls onto a clean tray. Seal in a plastic bag, freeze until firm and then put in labelled and dated plastic bags to reduce the amount of freezer space used. Seal well and remove single cubes as required. Never leave food cubes out of the freezer for any length of time until you are ready to use them.

■ For babies, fish can be frozen for up to 1 month, meat for up to 3 months, offal for up to 1 month, fruit and vegetables for up to 3 months and soups and baked goods for up to 6 months.

■ Plan meals on a weekly basis and buy fruit, vegetables and meat in larger quantities. Cook them for puréeing, mashing or chopping at one time and then freeze. Remember to keep two days' supply in the refrigerator and think ahead, transferring frozen portions to the refrigerator when supplies are running low.

■ Great care must be taken when using the microwave oven to heat food for your baby. Remember that food continues to cook for several seconds after the heating time is complete and is therefore very hot. Always test before serving.

hints

■ Always refer to the manufacturer's manual for microwave defrosting programmes. Loosen all covers and wraps and remove any metal ties before defrosting. For even defrosting, turn or stir food occasionally.

■ To reheat frozen baby foods, use a microwave or put in a dish over a saucepan of simmering water. The microwave is also ideal for cooking fruit and vegetables for puréeing.

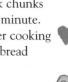

■ Always mix food thoroughly during and after heating, as the outside could be very hot while the inside is still cold. Leave it to stand for several minutes before serving.

■ Make your own teething biscuits by placing 6 thick chunks of bread in the microwave. Cook on High power for 1 minute. Allow to stand for 1 minute. If the biscuits need further cooking to dry out thoroughly (this will depend on the type of bread used), use short, 30-second bursts.

■ Cook baby portions of rice or pasta in the microwave oven—1/2 cup rice or pasta in a large microwave-safe casserole dish with 1 cup water. Cook on High power, uncovered, for 10 to 12 minutes.

■ When preparing food for the whole family, set aside your baby's serving before adding any spices or strong flavorings.

■ As babies like soft food, it is tempting to overcook fruit and vegetables. However, try not to do this and, if possible, use any cooking liquid for puréeing to help retain the nutrients.

■ Keep a supply of fruit (fresh and dried), teething biscuits, cheese, grated vegetables for snacks for older babies and toddlers.

PICNIC FOOD

Taking your toddler to the park or the beach? Make it a real day out with a portable packed lunch.

CHEESY PIZZA

Preparation: **15 minutes**
Cooking time: **20 minutes**
MAKES **12** WEDGES

2 cups self-rising flour
1 oz butter, chopped
1/2 cup milk
1/2 cup water

Topping:
1 cup grated cheese
1 tomato, finely chopped
1/4 cup ricotta cheese
1/4 cup chopped ham
1 tablespoon chopped parsley

1 Preheat the oven to 425°F. Sift the flour into a bowl and use your fingertips to rub in the butter until it looks like bread crumbs. Make a well in the center and pour in the combined milk and water.

2 Mix quickly into a soft dough and turn onto a lightly floured surface. Knead lightly. Press or roll out to a circle 1/2 inch thick.

3 Put the pizza base on an oiled baking sheet. Mix together all the topping ingredients and spoon over the pastry, leaving a border round the edge.

4 Bake for 20 minutes. Cut into slices and serve with salad.

MINI QUICHE LORRAINES

Preparation: **10 minutes**
Cooking time: **25 minutes**
MAKES APPROXIMATELY **12**

2 sheets frozen ready-
    rolled pie pastry
1 tomato, chopped
1/2 cup grated tasty
    cheese
1/4 cup chopped ham
    or bacon
1 green onion, finely
    chopped
1/2 cup milk
1 egg

1 Preheat the oven to 350°F. Cut the pastry into 12 rounds using a 3 inch cutter. Line 12 shallow tart pans with the pastry. Cut pieces of wax paper to cover each pastry shell. Fill with uncooked rice, chickpeas or baking beans and bake blind for 5 minutes. Remove the paper and rice, peas or beans and bake for a further 2 minutes. Cool before filling.

2 Mix together the tomato, cheese, ham and green onion and spoon into the pans.

3 Whisk together the milk and egg. Pour enough into each pan to cover the filling.

4 Bake in the oven for 15–20 minutes, or until the filling is set and golden.

5 Transfer to a wire rack to cool. Store in the refrigerator in an airtight container for up to two days.

SHORTBREADS

Preparation: **15 minutes**
Cooking time: **30 minutes**
MAKES **16** PIECES

2 cups all-purpose flour
2 tablespoons rice
  flour
1/2 cup sugar
8 oz butter,
  chopped

1 Preheat the oven
to 315°F. Sift the
flours together into a
large bowl and mix in
the sugar. Rub in the
butter using your
fingertips and press the
mixture together.

2 Turn out onto a
lightly floured
surface and knead
gently. Press out into a
round about 1/2 inch
thick and cut out
with shaped cutters.
Put onto greased
cookie sheets.

3 Bake for 25–30
minutes, or until
golden brown.

4 Leave to cool on the
trays for 5 minutes
and then transfer to a
wire rack to cool
completely. Store in an
airtight container.

From top: *Orange Cake;*
Scones; Shortbreads

SCONES

Preparation: **10 minutes**
Cooking time: **12 minutes**
MAKES ABOUT **12**

2 cups self-rising
  flour
1 oz butter, chopped
1/2 cup milk
1/2 cup water

1 Preheat the oven to
  425°F. Sift the flour
into a large bowl and
rub in the butter using
your fingertips.

2 Make a well in the
  center of the flour.
Pour in the combined
milk and water, saving
1 teaspoonful to glaze.
Mix quickly to a soft
dough with a knife.

3 Turn onto a lightly
  floured board and
knead lightly. Press or
roll out to form a round
about 1/2 inch thick.

4 Cut into rounds or
  wedges and put
close together on a
greased baking sheet.
Glaze with the reserved
milk and water mix.

5 Bake for 10–12
  minutes, or until the
scones sound hollow
when tapped. Cool on
a wire rack.

ORANGE CAKE

Preparation: **10 minutes**
Cooking time: **45 minutes**
MAKES **1** CAKE

4 oz butter
1/2 cup sugar
2 eggs
1 teaspoon vanilla
  extract
grated rind of 1 orange
2 cups self-rising
  flour, sifted
1/4 cup orange juice
1/4 cup milk

1 Preheat the oven
  to 350°F. Beat the
butter and sugar
together until light
and fluffy.

2 Add the eggs one at
  a time, beating well.
Beat in the vanilla
extract and rind.

3 Fold the flour into
  the mixture
alternately with the
combined juice and
milk, beginning and
ending with the flour.

4 Spoon the mixture
  into a greased and
floured 4 x 8 inch loaf
pan and bake for
40–45 minutes. Leave
to cool in the pan for a
few minutes, then turn
out onto a wire rack.

BANANA CAKE

Preparation: **10 minutes**
Cooking time: **45 minutes**
MAKES **1** LOAF

4 oz butter
$1/2$ cup brown sugar
2 eggs
1 cup mashed banana
   (about 3 ripe
   bananas)
$1/2$ cup sour cream
2 cups self-rising
   flour, sifted

Icing:
$11/2$ cups confectioners'
   sugar, sifted
$3/4$ oz soft butter
1 teaspoon grated
   lemon rind
1–2 tablespoons lemon
   juice

1 Preheat the oven to
350°F. Cream the
butter and sugar
together until fluffy.
Add the eggs one at a
time, beating well. Stir
in the mashed banana
and sour cream.

2 Lightly fold in the
flour. Spoon the
mixture into a greased
and lined 9 x 5 inch
loaf pan.

3 Bake for 40–45
minutes, or until a

skewer inserted into
the center comes out
clean. Turn onto a wire
rack to cool.

4 Mix together all the
icing ingredients
until smooth, then
spread over the cooled
cake. If necessary, the
cake can be wrapped in
freezer wrap and frozen.

DATE SQUARES

Preparation: **10 minutes**
Cooking time: **25 minutes**
MAKES ABOUT **24**

3 oz butter
$3/4$ cup brown sugar
1 egg
$11/2$ cups self-rising
flour, sifted
1 cup chopped dates

1 Preheat the oven to
350°F. Cream
together the butter and
sugar until well
combined. Add the
egg and beat well.

2 Gently fold in the
flour, followed by
the dates. Press gently
into a greased shallow
7 x 11 inch pan.

3 Bake for 20–25
minutes, or until
lightly golden brown.
Cut into squares.

MERINGUE SLICE

Preparation: **15 minutes**
Cooking time: **30 minutes**
MAKES ABOUT **24**

4 oz butter
1 cup sugar
2 eggs, separated
1 cup self-rising
   flour, sifted
1 cup shredded
   coconut

1 Preheat the oven to
350°F. Cream the
butter and half the
sugar together until
light and fluffy. Add
the egg yolks and beat.

2 Fold in the flour.
Flour your fingertips
and press the dough
into the base of a greased
7 x 11 inch pan.

3 Beat the egg whites
into stiff peaks.
Gradually beat in the
rest of the sugar until
thick and glossy. Fold
in the coconut.

4 Spread the meringue
over the pastry base.
Bake for 25–30
minutes, or until a
skewer comes out clean
when inserted into the
center. Cool, then cut
into squares. Store in
an airtight container.

From top: *Banana Cake; Meringue Slice; Date Squares*

TODDLER DINNERS

Dinner times become easier and much more fun when your toddler is able to join the family for meals.

....

CREAMY CHICKEN AND CORN SOUP

Preparation: **5 minutes**
Cooking time: **25 minutes**
MAKES ABOUT 4 CUPS

4 cups chicken stock
1 cup finely chopped cooked chicken
4¹/2 oz creamed corn
1/4 cup small pasta
1 tablespoon chopped parsley

1 Place the stock, chicken, corn and pasta in a pan. Bring to the boil and then reduce the heat and simmer for 15–20 minutes, or until the pasta is very tender.

2 Stir in the parsley and allow to cool. Process until smooth in a food processor or blender. Reheat or refrigerate in an airtight container for up to 5 days or freeze in portion sizes.

MINESTRONE

Preparation: **15 minutes**
Cooking time: **1**1/2 **hours**
MAKES 14 CUPS

....

2 tablespoons olive oil
1 onion, chopped
1 slice rindless bacon, finely chopped
10 oz mixed canned beans such as navy, chickpeas and lima, drained and rinsed
3 carrots, chopped
3 zucchini, sliced
2 stalks celery, sliced
2 potatoes, peeled and chopped
4 oz green beans, trimmed and sliced
14 oz can tomatoes
10 cups water
1/3 cup small pasta
grated Parmesan cheese
chopped parsley

1 Heat the oil in a large saucepan and sauté the onion and bacon until the onion

is tender. Add the beans, carrot, zucchini, celery, potatoes and tomatoes and cook, stirring, for 1 minute.

2 Add the water to the pan and season to taste with pepper and herbs of your choice. Bring to the boil and then reduce the heat and simmer, covered, for 1 hour.

3 Stir in the pasta and simmer for a further 15 minutes, or until tender. Sprinkle the Minestrone with cheese and parsley and serve with crusty bread.

> **Croûtons:** Cut the crusts from 4 slices of bread and cut the bread into cubes. Heat 1 oz butter and 1 tablespoon oil in a small frying pan. Add the bread in batches and fry, turning, until crisp and golden. Drain on paper towels. Store in an airtight container.

From top: *Creamy Chicken and Corn Soup; Minestrone*

▶

SIMPLE BOLOGNESE

Preparation: **10 minutes**
Cooking time: **30 minutes**
SERVES 8

2 tablespoons olive oil
1 onion, finely
   chopped
1 clove garlic, crushed
1 lb ground steak
1/4 cup chopped
   mushrooms
2 tablespoons tomato
   paste
14 oz can tomatoes,
   chopped
1/2 cup beef stock
   or water
1 tablespoon chopped
   parsley
seasoning, to taste
cooked pasta of choice

1 Heat the oil in a
   heavy-based pan and
sauté the onion and
garlic until tender. Add
the ground steak and
brown well, breaking up
with a spoon as it cooks.

2 Add the mushrooms
   and cook for 1
minute. Blend in the
tomato paste.

3 Stir in the tomatoes,
   stock, parsley and
seasoning. Bring to the
boil and then reduce

the heat and simmer,
stirring occasionally,
for 20 minutes.

4 Toss the sauce
   through hot,
drained pasta. Sprinkle
with grated Parmesan
or Cheddar, if desired,
and serve with salad.

Note: If you don't
have chopped canned
tomatoes, you can
use whole canned
tomatoes: chop them
in the can with a pair of
scissors or sharp knife.

CARROT AND POTATO SOUP

Preparation: **10 minutes**
Cooking time: **35 minutes**
SERVES 4

1/2 oz butter or 1
   tablespoon olive oil
3 carrots, chopped
1 potato, peeled and
   chopped
4 cups chicken or
   vegetable stock
milk

1 Melt the butter or
   oil in a medium-
sized saucepan. Add the
carrot and potato and
cook over low heat for
3 minutes.

2 Pour in the stock
   and bring to the
boil. Reduce the heat
and simmer for 25–30
minutes, or until the
vegetables are very
tender. Allow to cool.

3 Process the soup in
   a food processor or
blender until smooth.
Refrigerate in an
airtight container for
up to five days or freeze
in serving portions.
Reheat with a little
milk to taste.

TODDLER COMBO

Preparation: **10 minutes**
Cooking time: **25 minutes**
SERVES 2

1 potato, peeled and
   chopped
1 carrot, chopped
1 zucchini, chopped
1/2 cup chopped sweet
   potato
1/4 cup chopped green
   beans
1/2 cup chopped
   cooked meat

1 Steam, boil or
   microwave the
vegetables until tender
and then mix with the
meat to serve.

◄ **From top:** *Carrot and Potato Soup;*
Toddler Combo; Simple Bolognese

MACARONI CHEESE

Preparation: **5 minutes**
Cooking time: **10 minutes**
SERVES 4

1 oz butter
1 tablespoon all-purpose flour
1 cup milk
seasoning, to taste
1/2 cup grated cheese
2 cups cooked macaroni

1 Melt the butter in a small saucepan. Blend in the flour and cook for 1 minute.

2 Remove from the heat and gradually blend in the milk. Return to the heat and cook, stirring, until the sauce boils and thickens.

3 Reduce the heat and simmer for 3 minutes. Season and stir in the cheese. Mix the macaroni through the sauce and serve with tomato wedges.

Note: The mixture can be put into ramekins and topped with a little grated cheese and dry bread crumbs, then baked in a 350°F oven for 5–10 minutes or until golden. Allow the ramekins to cool before serving.

APRICOT CHICKEN

Preparation: **10 minutes**
Cooking time: **50 minutes**
SERVES 4–6

1 lb boneless chicken thighs, chopped, skin removed
4 oz mushrooms, sliced
1 onion, thinly sliced
1 1/2 oz packet chicken noodle soup
14 oz canned apricots in their own juice
4 oz green beans or snow peas, trimmed

1 Preheat the oven to 350°F. Place the chicken, mushrooms, onion, soup mix and apricots in a large casserole dish, cover and bake for about 45 minutes, or until the chicken is tender.

2 Stir in the beans or snow peas. Bake for a further 5 minutes and then serve with crusty bread and a salad.

Note: For young children, be very careful to remove any chicken skin and small bones which may cause choking.

VEGETABLE AND NOODLE STIR-FRY

Preparation: **10 minutes**
Cooking time: **5 minutes**
SERVES 4

2 teaspoons oil
1 carrot, chopped
1 stalk celery, chopped
1 small zucchini, sliced
$1/2$ bell pepper, seeded and chopped
$1/4$ cup cauliflower florets
$1/4$ cup broccoli florets
$1/4$ cup sliced green beans
$1^3/4$ oz cellophane or egg noodles
2 teaspoons soy sauce

1 Heat the oil in a wok or frying pan. Stir-fry the carrot, celery, zucchini, pepper, cauliflower, broccoli and beans for 2–3 minutes.

2 Place the noodles in a bowl. Cover with boiling water. Leave to stand for 1 minute, or until tender. Drain.

3 Toss the noodles through the vegetables with soy sauce. Stir-fry for 1 minute. Serve immediately.

Left to right: *Macaroni Cheese; Apricot Chicken; Vegetable and Noodle Stir-fry*

JUNIOR RISOTTO

Preparation: **10 minutes**
Cooking time: **20 minutes**
SERVES **2**

1 tablespoon olive oil
4 oz lean ground
   steak
1/4 cup chopped
   mushrooms
1 tomato, peeled,
   seeded and chopped
1/4 cup peas
1 tablespoon tomato
   ketchup
1/4 cup rice
1 cup chicken stock

1 Heat the oil in a
   small saucepan, add
the meat and brown
well. Add the
mushrooms, tomato,
peas and ketchup and
cook for 1 minute.
2 Stir in the rice, add
   the stock and bring
to the boil. Reduce the
heat and simmer,
covered, for 12 minutes
or until the rice is
tender and the stock is
all absorbed.

> **Hint:** To peel a
> tomato, cut a cross in
> the top, plunge in
> boiling water then into
> cold. The skin will peel
> away from the cross.

KIDDY CASSEROLE

Preparation: **10 minutes**
Cooking time: **1 hour**
SERVES **2**

1 tablespoon olive oil
1 small onion, finely
   chopped
8 oz beef or chicken
   trimmed and cut
   into small chunks
2 oz button
   mushrooms
1 potato, peeled and
   cut into chunks
1 carrot, chopped
1 zucchini, sliced
1 tomato, peeled and
   chopped
2 cups stock

1 Preheat the oven to
   350°F. Heat the oil
in a frying pan and
sauté the onion until
tender. Add the meat
or chicken and brown
well. Transfer the
mixture to a small
casserole dish.
2 Add all the
   remaining
ingredients to the
casserole dish and bake,
covered, for about
1 hour, or until the
meat is tender.

MINI POTATO AND PUMPKIN BAKES

Preparation: **10 minutes**
Cooking time: **30 minutes**
SERVES **4**

1 large potato, peeled,
   and thinly sliced
4 oz pumpkin, peeled
   and thinly sliced
1/2 cup milk
1/2 oz butter

1 Preheat the oven to
   350°F. Layer the
potato and pumpkin in
4 well-greased 1/2-cup
ramekins, cutting the
slices into rounds to fit.
2 Pour the milk into
   the ramekins and
place some small pieces
of butter on top.
3 Put the ramekins on
   a baking sheet and
bake for 30 minutes,
or until golden. Turn
out onto a plate to serve.

> **Note:** If you are
> cooking food for your
> toddler in a ramekin,
> always turn the food
> out onto a plate to
> serve or allow the
> ramekin to cool
> completely before
> giving to your child.

From top: *Junior Risotto; Kiddy Casserole;
Mini Potato and Pumpkin Bakes* ▶

MINI SHEPHERD'S PIES

Preparation: **10 minutes**
Cooking time: **30 minutes**
MAKES 4

1 tablespoon oil
1 lb ground steak
2 tablespoons all-purpose flour
1 cup beef stock
2 tablespoons chopped parsley
pepper, to taste
4 potatoes, peeled and cooked
1/4 cup milk
1/2 oz butter
2 cups frozen mixed vegetables, thawed (peas, beans, carrots)
1/2 cup grated cheese
1/4 cup dried bread crumbs

1 Preheat the oven to 350°F. Heat the oil in a frying pan, add the ground steak and brown, breaking it up with a spoon as it cooks. Stir in the flour and cook, stirring, for 1 minute.

2 Blend in the stock, parsley and pepper. Simmer, stirring, for about 5 minutes, or until the mixture thickens.

3 Mash the potatoes well and beat until smooth with the milk and butter, adding more of each if needed.

4 Spoon the meat mixture into four small ramekin dishes. Top with an even amount of vegetables and spread the mashed potato over the top.

5 Mix together the cheese and bread crumbs and sprinkle over each pie. Bake in the oven for 10–15 minutes, or until the tops are golden.

Note: Use chopped cooked meat (such as leftover roast) in place of ground steak.

PASTA BAKE

Preparation: **10 minutes**
Cooking time: **1 hour**
SERVES 4–6

8 oz pasta, cooked
  and drained
4 oz ricotta cheese
3 eggs
1 tablespoon olive oil
1 onion, chopped
1 lb ground steak,
  lamb, pork or
  chicken
14 oz can tomatoes,
  chopped
1/2 cup water
2 tablespoons tomato
  paste
10 fl oz cream
1 1/2 cups grated cheese
1/2 cup fresh
  bread crumbs

1 Combine the pasta with the ricotta and 1 egg. Press into a greased casserole dish.

2 Heat the oil in a pan and cook the onion until tender. Add the ground steak and brown well.

3 Stir in the tomatoes, water and tomato paste. Simmer, uncovered, for 15–20 minutes, or until the sauce begins to thicken, and then spoon over the pasta.

4 Whisk together the cream, remaining eggs and 1 cup cheese and pour over the meat mixture. Combine the remaining cheese and the bread crumbs and sprinkle over the top.

5 Bake at 350°F for 35–40 minutes, or until golden.

FAMILY CASEROLE

Preparation: **10 minutes**
Cooking time: **3 hours**
SERVES **4–6**

2¹/₂ oz butter
2 tablespoons oil
2 lb round steak, cut
    into 2 cm cubes
6 small onions
4 potatoes, peeled
    and halved
3 carrots, halved
2 parsnips, chopped
¹/₃ cup all-purpose flour
5 cups beef stock
¹/₄ cup tomato paste
1 teaspoon
    Worcestershire
    sauce
chopped parsley

1 Heat ¹/₂ oz butter with the oil in a large pan. Add the meat in batches and brown well on all sides. Remove to a plate.

2 Add the onions, potatoes, carrots and parsnips to the pan and cook until golden. Remove to the plate and cover with foil.

3 Add the remaining butter to the pan and stir in the flour. Cook, stirring, until golden brown and then remove from the heat.

4 Gradually blend in the stock, tomato paste, sauce, salt and pepper and return to the heat. Cook, stirring continuously, until the sauce boils and thickens.

5 Return the meat to the pan, stirring to coat it in sauce. Bring to the boil and then reduce the heat and simmer, covered, for 1¹/₂–2 hours.

6 Add the reserved vegetables. Simmer for 30 minutes, or until the vegetables are tender. Transfer the meat and vegetables to a serving plate and keep warm.

7 Bring the sauce to the boil and then reduce the heat and simmer, uncovered, until slightly thickened. Sprinkle the meat and vegetables with parsley and serve with sauce.

PASTA AND VEGETABLE GRATIN

Preparation: **10 minutes**
Cooking time: **30 minutes**
SERVES 2

1 cup chopped mixed
   vegetables
2 cups cooked pasta
1 oz butter
1 tablespoon all-
   purpose flour
1 cup milk
1/4 cup grated cheese
1 tablespoon dried
   bread crumbs

1 Preheat the oven to 350°F. Steam, boil or microwave the vegetables in a little water, until tender. Put in a greased casserole dish with the pasta and stir to combine.

2 Melt the butter in a small pan. Blend in the flour and cook, stirring, for 1 minute.

3 Gradually blend in the milk until smooth. Cook, stirring, until the sauce boils and thickens. Simmer for 3 minutes. Pour over the vegetables.

4 Mix together the cheese and bread crumbs and sprinkle over the top. Bake for 15 minutes.

PEAR CRUMBLE

Preparation: **5 minutes**
Cooking time: **40 minutes**
SERVES 4–6

4 pears, peeled, cored
  and sliced
1 tablespoon sugar
2 cups all-purpose or
  whole wheat flour,
  sifted
4 oz butter, chopped
1/2 cup brown sugar

1 Preheat the oven
  to 375°F. Place
the fruit in the base
of a greased ovenproof
dish and sprinkle
with sugar.

2 Put the flour in a
  bowl. Rub in the
butter with your
fingertips until the
mixture is crumbly. Stir
in the brown sugar.

3 Sprinkle the
  crumble topping
over the fruit. Bake for
35–40 minutes, or until
golden. Serve warm
with custard.

Note: Use apples
and rhubarb or other
fruit, or berries for
older toddlers. Try
adding a tablespoon
of coconut to the
crumble topping.

VANILLA ICE CREAM

Preparation: **5 minutes**
Cooking time: **15 minutes**
SERVES 4

1 cup milk
1 cup cream
1 teaspoon vanilla
  extract
2 eggs
2 egg yolks
1/2 cup sugar

1 Put the milk and
  cream in a small
saucepan. Bring to the
boil and then remove
from the heat. Stir in
the vanilla extract.

2 Whisk the eggs, egg
  yolks and sugar
together in a heat-
resistant bowl. Whisk
in the milk mixture.

3 Place the bowl over
  a saucepan of gently
simmering water and
whisk until the mixture
thickens and coats the
back of a metal spoon.

4 Pour the custard
  into a metal pan
and freeze until it is
semi-solid.

5 Beat the mixture
  thoroughly, either
in a food processor or
by hand, to remove the

ice crystals. Return to
the pan, cover with foil
and freeze until firm.
Serve with fruit, wafers,
toppings or in a cone.

Note: To make a
fruity ice cream, just
stir in 2 cups chopped
or puréed fruit after
processing the ice
cream and then freeze
until firm.

TRIFLE MAGIC

Preparation: **15 minutes**
Cooking time: **Nil**
SERVES 4

1 ready-made jelly
  roll, sliced
3 oz packet Jell-o,
  set in a tray
2 cups chopped fruit
1 cup prepared custard,
  or custard-style
  yogurt

1 Arrange the cake in
  the bases of small
serving dishes. Chop
the Jell-o roughly, mix
with the fruit and
spoon over the cake.

2 Pour over the
  custard and serve
with ice cream.

From top: *Vanilla Ice Cream;*
Trifle Magic; Pear Crumble ▶

fussy

Without warning your child may begin to refuse once-loved food. This is not necessarily a criticism of your culinary skills but just as likely to be his first assertion of individual choice. Don't panic—remember that he will always eat when he is hungry. Run through the following checklist to see if there is anything you can do to help.

■ Make sure meal times are happy and relaxed. If meal times become associated with anger they will become more stressful for both of you, with your baby even less inclined to eat. Don't insist that your child finishes everything. If he refuses food do not offer substitutes but wait until the next meal.

■ Are you still puréeing food when your older baby has progressed beyond that? Or overestimating his ability to chew by offering large solid pieces?

■ Children are creatures of habit. Keep meals to regular times and give him his own chair and utensils. If he seems unsettled and won't eat, consider if there have been any recent changes that have threatened his security.

■ Try disguising nutritious food your child has rejected by mixing it in with an old favorite such as mashed potatoes.

■ Serve small portions, giving seconds if they are asked for. Three small meals and two snacks daily suit most children better than three dauntingly large meals. Don't put too much on the plate and always try to make it look attractive.

■ Any child who is upset, tired, teething or not feeling well is unlikely to want to eat.

eaters

■ Remember that children have growth spurts. A baby grows a proportionately large amount in his first year but you will find that a 5-year old often only eats as much as a 1-year old.

■ Has your child been given snacks throughout the day? Too much milk or fruit juice will take the edge off any appetite. Two cups of orange juice are equivalent to four oranges.

■ Encourage his appetite through fresh air, exercise and sleep—perhaps he has been less active than usual and isn't as hungry.

■ Genuine dislikes are often formed early—if certain foods are always left on the plate or spat out, this may be a sign to avoid these for a while. Always try them again at a later date.

■ To encourage good eating habits, don't always serve a sweet dessert after a savory. Stick to one-course meals with desserts occasionally. Don't bribe children with sweet foods—this only makes them seem more special.

■ Most children are hungriest mid-afternoon. Don't let him fill up on cakes, biscuits and candy then but, if it is practical, serve the main meal of the day, with a snack at dinner time.

■ Encourage your toddler to take an interest in food by helping with the preparation. Talk about the food as you cook and let him add herbs and spices then taste for flavor. Offer a choice of food to make him feel grown-up.

■ For older toddlers, put home-made sandwiches into a bag that makes it look as if they've been bought, and custards into well-washed yogurt cartons.

SNACKS AND NIBBLES

Toddlers lead very busy lives... always rushing about
looking for something new to explore. Often children
need a quick snack to top up their energy levels.
Instead of letting them fill up on sugar and additives,
make your own healthy treats.

From top: *Yogurt Dip;
Crunchy Cheese Bites;
Bruschetta*

CRUNCHY CHEESE BITES

Preparation: **15 minutes**
Cooking time: **15 minutes**
MAKES ABOUT **20**

2 cups grated cheese
4 oz feta cheese,
   crumbled
1/4 cup ricotta cheese
1/4 cup chopped green
   onions
1 small tomato,
   chopped
1 egg, beaten
pepper, to taste
4 sheets ready-rolled
   puff pastry
beaten egg and milk,
   to brush

1 Preheat the oven to
   425°F. Combine the
cheeses, green onions,
tomato, egg and pepper
in a bowl.

2 Cut the pastry into
   rounds using a
4 inch cutter. Place
heaped teaspoons of
the mixture onto one
half of each round.

3 Fold the pastry over
   the filling to make
semi-circles, brush the
edge with a little egg
and press the edges
together firmly with a
fork to seal.

4 Place on a baking
   sheet and brush
with a little milk. Bake
in the oven for 10–15
minutes, or until puffed
and golden. Allow to
cool for at least 10
minutes before serving.

BRUSCHETTA

Preparation: **5 minutes**
Cooking time: **10 minutes**
MAKES ABOUT **12 SLICES**

1 Italian loaf, sliced
1/2 cup olive oil
8 oz cottage cheese
2 tomatoes, chopped
1 avocado, chopped

1 Preheat the oven to
   400°F. Arrange the
bread on an oiled
baking sheet and brush
liberally with oil.

2 Bake for 10 minutes,
   or until golden.
Cool and then store
the Bruschetta in an
airtight container until
it is needed.

3 Mix together the
   cottage cheese,
tomatoes and avocado.
Spread over the
Bruschetta or serve
with it as a dip.

YOGURT DIP

Preparation: **15 minutes**
Cooking time: **Nil**
MAKES **1 CUP**

2 small cucumbers,
   seeded and chopped
6 1/4 oz natural yogurt,
   drained
2 cloves garlic,
   crushed
1 teaspoon lemon juice
1 teaspoon chopped
   dill
1/2 teaspoon chopped
   mint

1 Wrap the cucumber
   in a clean dish
towel and squeeze out
the water.

2 Mix the cucumber
   with the yogurt,
garlic, lemon juice, dill
and mint. Serve with
small pieces of pita
bread, vegetables such
as cucumber or cherry
tomatoes, and even
sliced fruit.

Note: Don't give
young children hard
vegetables or fruit,
such as carrot or
apple, for dipping.
Pieces can easily
break off and lead to
choking. Always grate
hard food for young
children and toddlers.

PARTY FOOD

There are few events more exciting for toddlers than a party. Ask a friend to help and don't be too ambitious.

CHEESE TWISTS

Preparation: **10 minutes**
Cooking time: **10 minutes**
MAKES ABOUT **30**

2 sheets ready-rolled puff pastry
tomato ketchup or Marmite
1 cup grated Cheddar cheese

1 Preheat the oven to 425°F. Spread one sheet of pastry with tomato ketchup or Marmite and sprinkle with cheese.

2 Put the second piece of pastry on top and press the edges to seal.

3 Cut into $1/2$ inch strips, then cut each into three pieces. Twist and put on a lightly greased baking sheet.

4 Bake in the oven for about 10 minutes, or until golden and puffed. Cool on a wire rack.

CORNY NESTS

Preparation: **5 minutes**
Cooking time: **15 minutes**
MAKES 24

1 oz butter
2 tablespoons all-
    purpose flour
$^1/_2$ cup milk
$^1/_2$ cup cream
$4^1/_2$ oz creamed corn
$^1/_2$ cup chopped ham
24 small puff pastry
    shells

1 Melt the butter in a small saucepan. Add the flour and cook, stirring, for 1 minute.

2 Remove from the heat and gradually blend in the combined milk and cream. Return to the heat and cook, stirring constantly until the sauce boils and thickens. Simmer for 3 minutes.

3 Blend in the corn and ham and spoon into warm puff pastry shells (reheated according to the packet directions).

MEATBALLS

Preparation: **10 minutes**
Cooking time: **10 minutes**
MAKES ABOUT 60

1 lb sausage meat
1 lb ground steak
$1^1/_4$ oz packet French
    onion soup
$^1/_4$ cup tomato ketchup
2 tablespoons chopped
    parsley
2 tablespoons oil

1 Mix together the sausage, steak, soup mix, ketchup and parsley. Wet your hands to prevent sticking and then mold the mixture into balls.

2 Heat the oil in a frying pan. Add half the meatballs, tossing over medium heat for about 5 minutes, or until cooked through.

3 Drain well on crumpled paper towels and repeat with the remaining balls. Serve warm.

Left to right:
Corny Nests;
Cheese Twists;
Meatballs

BABY ECLAIRS

Preparation: **15 minutes**
Cooking time: **40 minutes**
MAKES ABOUT 24

2¹/2 oz butter
1 cup all-purpose flour
4 eggs
4 oz dark chocolate,
   melted
whipped cream

1 Preheat the oven to 400°F. Put the butter in a pan with 1 cup water. Bring to the boil; sift in all the flour.

2 Cook, stirring, until the mixture forms a ball. Transfer to a bowl and cool for 5 minutes.

3 Add the eggs, one at a time, beating well until thick and glossy. Spoon into a piping bag with a plain nozzle and pipe short lengths onto a greased baking sheet. Sprinkle with a little water.

4 Bake for 10–15 minutes. Reduce the oven to 350°F and bake for a further 10–15 minutes, or until golden and firm.

5 Pierce the side of each éclair with a skewer to allow steam to escape. Turn off the oven and leave the éclairs inside for about 5 minutes to dry out. Cool on a wire rack.

6 Split the éclairs in half lengthways and remove any uncooked pastry. Spread the tops with chocolate, allow to set, fill with cream and replace the tops.

CHOCOLATE SPONGE

Preparation: **10 minutes**
Cooking time: **20 minutes**
MAKES 1 CAKE

3 eggs, separated
³/4 cup sugar
1 cup self-rising
   flour, sifted
2 oz chocolate, melted
3 tablespoons water

1 Preheat the oven to 350°F. Grease a deep 8 inch round or square cake pan and dust with flour. Beat the egg whites in a clean dry bowl until stiff peaks form. Beat in the sugar until thick and glossy.

2 Beat in the egg yolks. Gently fold in the flour and then the chocolate and water.

3 Pour into the pan and bake for 15–20 minutes, or until the cake springs back when pressed. Cool on a wire rack. Decorate with cream, jam or butter cream or as a party cake (pages 62–63).

BUTTER CREAM

Beat 4 oz butter until creamy and gradually add 1¹/2 cups sifted confectioners' sugar. Beat until thick and smooth. Leave plain or color and flavor with melted chocolate, orange or lemon juice, food coloring etc.

MERINGUES

Preheat the oven to 300°F. Line a baking sheet with foil or baking paper. Beat 3 egg whites until stiff. Gradually blend in ¹/2 cup sugar until thick and glossy. Fold in ¹/3 cup sugar and spoon or pipe small mounds onto the baking sheet. Bake for 1 to 1¹/2 hours, or until dry. Cool and store in an airtight container.

From top: *Chocolate Sponge topped with cream; Baby Eclairs; Meringues* ▶

BUNNY CAKE

8 inch square sponge
  cake (page 60)
2 quantities butter
  cream (page 60)
pink food coloring
2 plain, sweet cookies
1 large white
  marshmallow, cut
  horizontally in half
2 brown M & Ms
2 colored candy
  laces
1 licorice whip
2 white mini
  marshmallows

1 Cut the cake in half.
  Cut one piece in
half again. Put the long
piece and one of the
quarters together to
make a number 1.

2 Cut the remaining
  piece of cake in half
again and place at the
base to make feet. Cut
the ends of the feet to
round them a little.
Leave a small portion
of butter cream white
and tint the rest pink.

3 Stick the pieces of
  cake together with
butter cream. Spread
the rest over the cake
and over the cookies to
make ears as shown.
Decorate the bunny's
face with the candy
as shown.

Note: Although it is
tempting at parties,
  don't give young
  children hard candy,
  nuts or popcorn—they
  can easily lead to
  choking. Make sure
  toddlers sit quietly,
  rather than running
  around or playing
  while they eat.

FARMYARD CAKE

8 inch square sponge
  cake (page 60)
1 1/2 quantities butter
  cream (page 60)
1/2 cup shredded
  coconut, toasted
green and brown food
  coloring
chocolate sticks
chocolate pretzels
2 rectangular
  chocolates for feed
  bins
shredded coconut
miniature farmyard
  figures

1 Trim the sides of the
  cake and cover with
butter cream, roughing
up the surface.

2 Put 2 tablespoons of
  coconut in a plastic
bag with 2–3 drops
brown coloring; shake to
combine. Repeat with
the remaining coconut
and green coloring.

3 Sprinkle the green
  coconut over the
cake and brown coconut
around the outside edge.
Put chocolate sticks in
the corners as fence
posts. Use the chocolate
pretzels to make fences.
Arrange the feed bins,
animals and gate.

CLOCK CAKE

8 inch round sponge
  cake (page 60)
1 quantity butter
  cream (page 60)
blue food coloring
lots of M & Ms
fruit roll-ups
2 different colored
  gummi worms
1 colored candy for
  clock center.

1 Tint the butter
  cream to a bright
blue and cover the cake.
Arrange the M & Ms
around the side.

2 Use a small sharp
  pair of scissors to cut
the numbers from the
fruit roll-ups and put
on the cake.

3 Use the gummi
  worms to make the
hands of the clock,
pointing them to the
child's age. Put the
candy in the center of
the cake.

Index